Guide To Emergency Cash

Generating Cash During Emergency

Contents

Introduction 1
How you can Handle a Cash Crisis 1
Learning to Handle a cash Emergency 2
    To be Calm is the very first Key to Managing a Money Emergency 3
    Moment to Crunch some Numbers 3
    The concept is Making an intelligent Decision and not really a Rash one 4
Increase your Cash Flow without Going Further into Debt 5
    Nowhere to go but up 5
Begin Building Your Emergency Fund 6
To build your Emergency Fund 8
Say Goodbye to Credit Cards 9
    One of the greatest methods to cut costs probably the fastest is to cut up many of those costly credit cards. 9
Here are a few great ideas for budget trimming that will work for only about everyone: 9
Remember, also, which you'll be teaching your children in order to be frugal and also to build great spending habits. 10
Painless Ways to Find Money for an urgent situation 10
Everyday Ways to Cut Costs for an Emergency 13
Much more Creative Ways to Save Money 15
    Thrifty Ways to Save Money 18
    Quite possibly YOU can save while on a shoestring 22
Which One Simple Word - Savings 22
What's your EMERGENCY PLAN? 23
    Isn't it time TO START A very good SAVINGS PLAN? 23
Smart Tips for Living on a Budget 27

Some suggestions to help you save: 31
Seven Serious Ways to Cut costs - Not for the Faint of Heart 32
What could be the answer? 33
The important thing on health that is fiscal is Stop Spending 34
    Much more Serious Savings Strategies 34
Make Small Cuts for Savings that are Huge 36
Emergency Money Strategy while Coping with Debt, Financial Family and Stress 40
    YOU Have TO HAVE your WITS ABOUT RAISING EMERGENCY MONEY 41
    Getting Fast Cash through Borrowing 43
A Few Timely Lessons in Simple Living 44
Better Money Management Thinking 44
Each day Money Saving Tips 45
    How you can Cut costs on Gas 45
Simpler Solutions for Managing your Money 48
Pay your Bills Online and Save 49
Reward Yourself 50
Several ways to reap the benefits of a Year-end Bonus 51
A couple of Useful Savings Strategies 54
Basic Ways to Bring both Calm AND Savings to your Life 54
Great WAYS TO FIND FREE MONEY 58
Making use of Good Commonsense and Planning - You Can Survive!! ... 62

Introduction

A time when the need is great and the resources are few comes at least once in the life of a human. It can be hard enough to make ends meet on a good salary, but a person can easily despair when times get rough and the money just isn't there to meet the need.

One hundred and one ways have been written with you in mind to collect emergency funds. This imaginative eBook will totally thrill you if you are just trying to come up with innovative ways to raise and save more.

If an individual can have good financial management and a good action plan, then they can then sleep better at night should emergency funds be required.

To come up with on-the-spot emergency cash, there is no real magic formula. There is a good deal of thought about and putting into effect a good idea. You've got it made, if you can do that. That is something any of us can do to make sure tomorrow is safe.

How you can Handle a Cash Crisis

Here's how to evaluate the condition and get back on your feet if you are hit with a major financial problem and you find yourself running around for emergency money.

Suddenly and without warning, the roof starts leaking! Your hot water heater shuts down and your machine goes up in flames, the clutch has to be fixed in your car, and within the same week, your son plans to have his wedding on Oahu Island!

You get a friendly letter from the IRS stating that you miscalculated your taxes in 1996 and that they now own your house while you wait, shocked and pondering an escape plan.

Your urgent focus needs this kind of money emergency

What're you doing?

The above scenario looks like an emergency of biblical proportions of money. For fear of finding a swarm of locusts, you are terrified of opening your front door!

Thank God, without having to sell your very soul, there are things you can already do to regain your financial life and equilibrium and maybe even ward off potential misfortune.

Learning to Handle a cash Emergency

Wherever financial woes remain, you should be confident of finding a crushing mental loss. You might as well start planning for the catastrophic fiscal and emotional fallout that is likely to come by stopping anything you try. If you intend to make a strong financial comeback, you will need to deal very well with both.

It will be your ability to cope with the individual pitfalls that will keep you in good stead if a money emergency hits. It is when a series of financial hits come the way where the burden begins to mount and make it even harder to deal with your life.

When you can logically and rationally look at each particular dilemma as it occurs, you will not be so confused. If you sit back and wring your hands in concern and cause all your emergencies to pile into one, you're going to find yourself down for the count.

Relaxation must take center stage. The comfort of panic you could NEVER give yourself. No one is there for you to just take over. You are all you've got.

The more you worry, the less effective you'll be. To be able to sit down and come up with an adequate strategy, you need to have a very calm mind. Be mindful of your propensity to further undermine your plans. You will be prepared to get to where you need to be and only conquer it only when you are at the calmest.

To be Calm is the very first Key to Managing a Money Emergency

It's crucial not to act right away, except at the first sign of a cash emergency. You will inevitably make an error if you do so! First, you have to control your feelings so you can manage your money again. Before you can even attempt to make a strategy, you simply must restore your equilibrium.

If your cash emergency allows you to act fast, try finding the advice of a debt counselor, finance coach, or financial advisor first. Whenever practicable, think about finding the help of a friend or family member who is financially sensitive who can help you come to a better viewpoint.

Know the adage that "two heads are better than just one at all times!" If you're strapped, you won't need to make a big cash commitment. Look for a planner who will supply you with a $150 one-hour consultation. This will also be what you need to safely turn the corner.

Moment to Crunch some Numbers

In order to maintain financial stability, the first step is to step back, take a deep breath, and analyze the damage. Perhaps one of the bigger mistakes people make is not being able to make a reasonable determination of where they are at when they are in a financial crisis.

You will get confused quickly. Two significant reasons, however, serve to sum up the hurt. First of all, you ought to know just how much you owe, how much money you've got in your wallet, and what it takes to bridge the difference between the two. Second, you'll want to stop all other mishaps, such as fines, more fixes, deadlines missing, etc.

If you're not prepared enough, you have to get ready on the spot. You will be caught unaware of some form of monetary crisis and you will feel cornered. Wouldn't it be perfect for the crisis to be ready and waiting? How possible is this, however to happen to you?

The bulk of people would be very prepared, at least. If the situation isn't too serious, they'll be able to handle it all right. Some are going to be sunk from the get-go. No matter how little or how many, the idea is not to be overwhelmed and to have a clear course of action. To cope with any sizable loss, you need to be thoroughly trained.

Ideally, the funds in the Unusual Expenses account in any good budget will compensate for such unforeseen expenses. Unfortunately, however, a popular topic is still present. You might well have an emergency stash, but it is drained most frequently. The majority of us are afflicted by this same problem, so take heart.

Many individuals make the mistake of turning to plastic for relief right around this time. This one, resist. You're just going to move the concerns from one pocket to the other.

On the other side, if you're sure you can tackle a cash emergency with credit cards, you'd better be sure you can pay them off when the time comes. Otherwise, why would you add another debt and another issue? It'll all catch up with you finally.

Try taking out a home equity line of credit if you're really running while on the last leg. For others, this will work. Income is tax-free, so it's not fixed-rate interest. However, be smart about this remedy. It will end up costing you more than you expected especially if you have already drained your own equity unless you intend to pay back the sum you lent promptly.

The concept is Making an intelligent Decision and not really a Rash one

Before investing from your 401(k) or IRA, thought well. There are exemptions that encourage you to do so but there are hidden costs as well without taking into account future taxation, fines, and other implications. Bear in mind that you'd have to reimburse the debt automatically if you were to lose your employment, or be charged as if it was a withdrawal. In the long term, this remedy may be very expensive.

Increase your Cash Flow without Going Further into Debt

Carry on a hobby you can turn into dollars. Can you walk a dog in the neighborhood? Weaving a teaching basket? Dining room host? Honey-sit for your sister's children? Can you do computer graphics? Take into account which of the strengths could be worth a few extra bucks and then go out and do it.

- Taking part-time jobs. The holidays are coming up fast, and many persons are adding part-time shopping work to their incomes. Only don't waste any of it on travel presents and make sure you bring it into your accounts.
- Invest more wisely. Many of us have our own ways of wasting dollars. Now see if you can delete the ones you're not going to miss. Save only the dollar you would usually spend on your cup of coffee adds up every day.
- Borrow from a friend or family who is trusted. The interest rate is low to zero, the cash is quick, but there is also greater remorse. Even before you meet them, make sure you have a proposal on how you are going to pay back the loan.

<u>Nowhere to go but up</u>

In your milk, you might waste your precious time crying about why you were picked out in this manner, or you can get busy and look at how this could have happened to you in the first place. If you want to stop future financial crises, you'll need to face some touchy reactions.

Suffering from a severe financial recession is a perfect moment for self-assessment. Tell yourself where you have gone wrong, where you are not paying attention, and how you might set yourself up for potential financial losses. If the same happens to you, learning the answers to these significant questions will help you out next time around.

Before the crisis begins, be prepared. Any time a financial burden falls in your face, you may not be able to predict it however, if you want to be cushioned against it you have to anticipate the unforeseen.

Be very vigilant. There is an emergency fund set aside for . . Emergency conditions. On a whim for every month, it is not intended to be exhausted. In the past few months, have a good look at your spending, because if you have had to lean heavily on your emergency account to pad your budget, it's time to reconsider your money management challenges and hurry.

Take extra heed. Take a leaf from this lady's journal... she found her towels were singing mildly when one day she pulled them out of the dryer. She brushed it off instead of calling the repairman before the next load caused her whole house to go up in flames. We all have these same moments when, before it's all too late, we see a future disaster hovering on the horizon and do nothing. Pay heed to the finer information and discourage global calamities from occurring.

Planning ahead more. Every 80,000 miles or so, the clutch is inevitably going to give out. Every 15 to 20 years, the roof could give way. In as many as five, a vacuum cleaner may give up the dust. Avoid the simple, and later pay unnecessarily. It's your calling.

It's getting creaky on your five-year-old laptop. You should wait until it dies. It would, however, expire at the worst possible moment, according to Murphy's Law of Money. Anyway, it might not be part of the budget to spend on a new machine, but planning ahead gives you more leverage on whether the hit is taken. Start preparing now, come hell or high water, for what you know is coming. For the unexpected, prepare smartly.

Begin Building Your Emergency Fund

It can be very hard to locate funds during an emergency if you forget to prepare. Establish emergency savings both in good and in poor times. The probability is very high that when you least foresee it you will be called upon to set up a sum of money on the spot.

Socking off three or six months of living costs is a really safe rule of thumb. When you are faced with big, unplanned expenditures such as a car that breaks down or desperately needed college funds, you can still use this same money.

The purpose of this form of investment strategy is to regularly put the cash aside, and then dig into it for actual emergencies. The effectiveness of this kind of long-range savings strategy would depend less on the return rate than on moving the money aside, day-by-day, and then leaving it there for a real emergency.

Lock it then and away conceal the key element.

Those working on a fixed budget are likely to have the hardest time putting up cash for emergencies. It's worth doing if you can manage to easily squeeze out another $10 or $20 per month and sock it away into a money market account.

Look at whether you can expect to lose per month from your existing income if you determine you need $2,000 in an emergency fund, and then look at that amount of money as a bill to support yourself. Decide on a monthly amount and then every month set the same amount aside and then watch it rise.

You will now be in the habit of setting aside an extra defined sum every month until you have achieved your target of $2,000. Continue to do so.

The thought of approaching your emergency fund like a bill is shared by financial advisors. Each month, put the money aside, but don't be fooled by the new offer. You should not touch the number, except in an emergency.

Financial planners echo the thought of treating your emergency fund as a bill. Put the money away every month, but do not be enticed by the newest purchase. You're not to touch the total, except for in an urgent situation.

It is difficult to set money away on your own. Retirement savings are effective because the money transfers out of your paycheck before you can get your hands on it and because early withdrawals entail taxes and fines.

Stashing money away takes patience in an easy-to-access money market portfolio. Limit the connections you have to the Emergency Fund. You will gain access to any of the money directly, but not any of it. The majority of the budget would, simply speaking, be reserved for emergencies and nothing more.

Shift one month of expenses to a one-month CD until you have saved up about two months of living expenses. Roll the principal and profit into another one-month-old CD as the CD matures. This way, the investments will increase well.

You will soon have another month of living costs that can be used to save in a two- to the three-month CD while you begin making periodic contributions to the emergency fund money market account. If you plan to put aside six months of costs, continue the process before a six-month CD can be bought easily. This way, the savings will grow easily.

To build your Emergency Fund

The first step in creating an emergency fund is to find out exactly how much money you have to set together in the first place before you start stashing away your money for an emergency.

People just don't know where their money is being invested. It's a lot easier to know whether you can scale down and continue to invest if you can pay for every cent.

You can't really prepare for crises, but building the fund as soon as possible is more important.

Say Goodbye to Credit Cards

One of the greatest methods to cut costs probably the fastest is to cut up many of those costly credit cards.

Perhaps one of the costliest types of money is credit cards. A very simple rule of thumb is don't use the cards on something you can either eat or wear until you pay off your credit card bills per month.

The restructuring of your debt is another successful rule of thumb. Why not fold them into a home equity loan if you have many credit cards, each at various interest rates, and then write off the interest payments? This is a good place for an emergency savings fund to launch.

Here are a few great ideas for budget trimming that will work for only about everyone:

If interest prices are particularly poor, try refinancing your mortgage and your car loans, too, while you're at it.

See how you can get away in one vehicle instead of two because you live in a city that has decent public transit.

Let it last for your new car. With sufficient maintenance, instead of every three years, you will be able to substitute it every six to eight years.

Do a periodic audit of the house's energy. Replace the necessities and renew the weather stripping, such as broken storm glass.

Cancel magazine subscriptions or newspapers that you don't read.

Eat out less often and learn to use leftovers to be innovative. If you stop at the nearest Deli for a morning cup of coffee, make coffee at home.

It cut down on the children's weekly allowance. Explain to them that for it to work, any family member has to donate to the emergency fund.

Remember, also, which you'll be teaching your children in order to be frugal and also to build great spending habits.

Saving money on your own offers many benefits, and it gets better over time, like most other items. In the end, the whole family will have peace of mind that comes with the understanding that you have built up and ready financial support for when things are the worst. When you need the most comfort as a family, the sacrifices you make today will be realized.

Painless Ways to Find Money for an urgent situation

If scooping up the change that falls between the cushions is your strategy for money for your next disaster, you may want to come up with a plan to add to that stash. To get a little extra green for the lean times is still a smart thing. Rainy days could be just around the corner. Funds for rainy days are required! Here are some really wise and basically painless ways to set some money away now!

Put a big packet, cookie box, jar of coffee, or something close aside. Throw a handful of bucks aside at the end of the week. You should have enough spare cash set together at the end of the first month to get a good start on an emergency fund. Don't count it or waste it on the thought of doing this. Place it away somewhere that's hidden. Place it somewhere where you won't be tempted to immerse yourself in it. This kind of capital is truly piling up!

Tip yourself the next time you treat yourself or your family to a dinner out! Just like you are going to tip the waitress 15 to 20 percent, set away for yourself the same number. Stash it safely in your cookie jar when you get done. Put a dollar away for the cookie jar. the time you go through a fast-food store, too!

When you get a decent boost the next time, instead of adding it to your living expenses, bank it! You'll only be living one increase behind this way and your bank account will expand by around 3%.

Take advantage of the option for cashback! Ask for a tiny amount of cashback the next time you make a payment with your debit card. Stash it safely in your cookie jar instead of spending it! Chances are you won't even lose the additional $1, $2, or $5 bills and you'll note how the number has stacked up as emergency time arrives.

Next time you pay off the big-ticket thing like a new car or tuition, keep making your own payments! Set up a savings account and slip the ghost payment into it every month. See as it builds beautifully.

Allocate the savings to your cookie jar if you have found you can get a cheaper long-distance calling contract and you want to switch. You're definitely not going to lose that little bit of extra revenue, because you're going to get a decent phone plan, too.

Consider attending a club for Christmas. You're going to save lots of money. You set away a little cash every year and put it into a hamper scheme. Then, you don't need to hunt around for Christmas cheer to share with your family as Christmas rolls around. With all sorts of festive treats, you paid for over the past year, your hamper comes packed to the max. This way, you can conveniently set away $50 per year for your emergency fund and you and your family can enjoy a Christmas free of hassle.

Sign up for a membership card for food shopping. You can see a print out at the bottom of your supermarket receipt that states how much you save per week. It truly adds up. On each weekly shopping drive, you can comfortably save an average of $15. Apply that amount to your savings cookie jar per week.

Did you spend this year with your tax refund? You really did it we all did it. That is because of the current laws on taxes. After April 15, several individuals will have a little extra money going their way. Decide to promptly deposit the additional money into your bank account or cash it and then stash it. Sure, you can come up with a lot of opportunities to spend the money today, but you can put it away later. Maybe you'll need it even later.

Take out a credit card that rewards your loyalty if you are a conscientious spender. Use a card that promises a cash payout when you pay off the bill each month, and deposit the cash. Using your incentive credit card smartly and your rainy-day fund will end up with a really good windfall.

Put a big mouthful of a jar in the kitchen aside. Your parents and grandparents are also likely to have had one. Simply clear your pockets or wipe out your change bag at the end of each workday. The shift all goes into the box. Who needs to bear all of the dead weight around anyway? A lot sooner than you thought, the spare change adds up. If you are at it at the end of each week, add at least one bill to your change jar. Just shoot for $20!

Is it time for that disgusting habit of smoking to give up? Just imagine the money that you'll save! If you are not yet able to leave, cut back by half at least. Place the savings in your change jar per day and watch it overflow!

Turn it into a coin-operated laundry. Hold a jar between your washer and dryer, and drop a coin or two any time you go to do a load of laundry. Month by month, this adds up.

The next time you go in on time to return a video rental, pocket the late fee yourself. You're going to see how easily $1.50 to $4 will add up.

If you want to shed more weight, try to compensate yourself with the expense of the product you do without every day. Place the money in your container for cash. You're going to look amazing and save yourself for a rainy day!

Place your telephone in a big jar. To make a call, everybody has to drop a coin. The funds are now going to the Emergency Fund. This one is functioning!

Everyday Ways to Cut Costs for an Emergency

There are a decent variety of means of saving your precious pennies when you think about it. Such strategies will entail some sacrifice, while others will take no consideration beforehand.

The point is to be careful of saving those spare pennies forever and you would have saved up a tidy amount before you know it.

- Spend less money than each week you earn.
- Hunt for a career with better wages.
- Keep your career skills sharp and up-to-date so that you can be on your toes and first in line when a new challenge pops up.
- Change your lifestyle such that you can invest a little less.
- To promote saving, build a firm financial budget.
- When you have to carry or break up credit cards that you can do without.
- If you have to use credit cards, pay all of them in full per month.
- Consolidate at once if you have credit card loans at elevated prices.
- Find out a way to lower interest on the student loan.
- Only say NO to cash spending wherever possible.
- Lower the costs, one by one.
- Stop buying things you can do without.
- Purchasing non-essential products from Forego.
- Refinance at a significantly cheaper cost on your mortgage or loan.
- At a much lower rate of interest, refinance your car loan.
- Find lower insurance rates/switch over then.
- Using coupons for shopping. Without a discount coupon, do not buy it.
- Wait for stuff to go on sale first before buying. Take account of vouchers for catalog saving.
- Do not purchase an item simply because it's on sale.

- Purchase as much as possible in generic or non-name brand merchandise.
- Wait for rates before purchasing to collapse to a reduced rate (in particular for electronic items).
- Reward yourself for saving money. Enjoy the shrinking of your debt and the expansion of your savings.
- Drive old or rented vehicles instead of brand new cars.
- Reducing the premiums on cars.
- Do not go out as much as you would like.
- Buy gift cards for half-price meals while you eat out.
- Buy discounted magazines only.
- Do more to sit at home during events.
- To gain even more, spend the cash you save.
- Build a schedule (as much as you can manage) to save $200 per month. Never skip the monthly savings payout and continue to find ways to raise it.
- Do not waste cash simply because you've got it.
- Look at achieving higher quality education.
- Keep really busy. You're going to have less time to spend money.
- To fill your time and stop you from wasting money, find an enjoyable hobby.
- Find a hobby that can be turned into profits.
- Avoid smoking and save money.
- Going on a reasonable diet and gaining weight. You're going to save money on food, look and sound healthier, and the healthcare expenses, in the long run, are going to decline significantly.
- Look closely at how you spend your money to save it.
- Study how your money should be handled through reading financial publications.
- Increase the amount of cash you receive from a second career, promotion, new jobs, savings, etc.
- Do not seek to contend with your neighbors and relatives. For what you have, be happy.
- Do not equate yourself with your neighbors and colleagues. Be satisfied where you are.
- Sell the auto and if possible, ride the bus to work.

- ❖ Contribute the limit to your 401K or an IRA per year.
- ❖ Before you use it, buy Dental Insurance.
- ❖ Before you use them, buy life insurance.

A way to save money is also to pay off your loans (it protects you from a debt payment and gets you closer to making money to invest).

To lower the telephone bill, turn.

Deleting pay channels or flipping to the satellite will lower the cable bill.

Earn additional money online by conducting brief surveys.

At all stages, maintain discipline.

When bargain hunting, be careful.

Today, start saving money!

Don't give up — just set aside $10 today!

Much more Creative Ways to Save Money

- ❖ Shop in thrift shops (especially for young children) for clothes. For 1/10 the price of new (or less), look for lightly aged or even new clothing.
- ❖ Pay the bills remotely. It's protected and you can use stamps to save it.
- ❖ Instead of taking them to school, put your children on the school bus.
- ❖ Slipcover or reupholster older furniture instead of purchasing costly new furniture for a simple refresh.

- Refinish and/or decorate furniture with fresh color. Create a custom piece utilizing older and broken furniture.
- Bring your normal lunch to work! Cook your meals in bulk and then freeze them to save still more space in smaller containers.
- Purchase a bread machine to bake your own bread. This one is a lot cheaper than $2.00 a loaf, and tastes fantastic!
- Shop at salvage retail stores for dented canned products and expired toiletries.
- Read paper magazines at the library or purchase them for .25 to .50 at the thrift store after everyone else has read them.
- Avoid drinking pricey sodas and just make decaffeinated iced tea or Kool-Aid.
- Cancel costly telecommunications solutions, such as waiting for calls.
- Instead of ordering pricey new novels, check out library books.
- Do not spin twice while you wash your hair every day. Shampoo saves!
- Modify your dietary habits and eliminate pricey, packaged foods.
- To keep your doctor's bills down, walk, and eat well.
- To keep the dentist's bill down, clean, and floss your teeth.
- Keep up with scheduled vehicle servicing to prevent expensive repairs.
- Instead of ordering new clothing, mend your clothes.
- Purchase only clothes that do not need dry cleaning.
- Take note of the nails you own. Only skip manicures.
- Wear a hairdo that does not need any upkeep. Ease the hairstyle.
- Get at least 3-6 quotations on products over $100 while shopping.
- Establish self-control and if possible, simplify your life.
- Purchase just cheap, no-name cosmetics from the drugstore.
- Break the sheets for the dryer in two.
- Where practicable, purchase generic over the counter medication rather than name brand products.
- Buy generic wipes, bottles, and milk for babies, anything you can for the infant.
- Check-in more wealthy neighborhoods for affordable, name-brand clothes at yard sales.

- Find trendy clothes in shops like the Void and Stitches distribution offices.
- Keep in style by finding simple colorful tees and skirts and incorporating cheaper, chic accessories.
- Purchase private baby clothes from someone who has an older child (one year older) than yours. This way you can find good quality garments cheaper.
- Place money in the piggy bank when you get cashback from a buy. Often send the entire dollar to the cashier, not the same sum. You will have "found" funds after a few months and can be used for an emergency fund.
- In the "bulk food" aisles in your grocery store, you can save money by shopping for groceries.
- In winter, bulk up. In winter, you don't need heat above 68 degrees inside your home. When in the kitchen, wear comfortable clothing and socks/slippers.
- Using all of the plastic bags you get for garbage bags at the grocery store.
- Any grocery stores, if you carry your own containers, give you a 5-cent credit per bag. Over time, pennies add up.
- Renting for possession instead of purchasing a new home. The fees are less costly.
- Have a water softener installed. Starting up can be pricey, but you use less shampoo/conditioner on your hair in the long run and it protects your appliances (pipes, iron, washing machine, dishwasher, kettle, and hot water tank) from limescale clogging up.
- Breastfeed your babies!
- Save money by remembering to search the lower items closest to the street level while shopping next time at the store, since they are always much cheaper than those at eye level. Often, fight the urge to buy extra things like magazines and snack bars at the checkout.
- Re-gift anytime you get a gift that you are sure you will not need! Next time you have to buy a present, giving one of your own free.
- Purchase, kill, and butcher your own calf. The quality of beef is an average of $1.00 per pound.

- Hand-pick your own in-season fruits and vegetables. These are inexpensive and higher quality ingredients.
- Wait to see it on DVD at the video store the next time you yearn to see a movie.
- Quick braking, cornering, and accelerating (speeding) can dramatically chew up the petrol. Never let your petrol needle go below a 1/2 tank or fill it up to "Empty" while operating it. Diming your gas tank and nickel gets you nowhere quick!

Thrifty Ways to Save Money

When you make a strong effort to regularly set money away, planning for an emergency does not need to be a hassle. Be in a spending mood and listen as it accumulates in that bank account.

- Save money by trading with family and friends instead of ordering a new DVD. Do the rounds once a month and you will have a new library of decent movies to watch before you know it.
- Every season, plant a small garden with all the vegetables that you really want. Even a little effort every day will save you dollars normally spent on the produce market for fresh vegetables.
- At the nearest thrift bread shop, buy your bread and other bakery items.
- Check for the newest DVD/video launches in the nearest library and then borrow three for $2.00 for two days.
- Learn the daily newspapers remotely.
- Scan eBay for high ticket products and then save hundreds on laptops, DVD players, etc. basically.
- Keep track of the expense of things that you purchase a lot to find them at the cheapest store, such as Family Dollar cleaning products, Wal-Mart pet food, etc.
- Make a concerted attempt to mix activities that involve somewhere to go, so you can get the best out of your mileage.

- Submit e-mail cards for holidays, birthdays, and thank you cards to your friends and relatives who do not feel slighted by this. In comparison, rather than calling long distance, e-mail relatives and friends who live far away.
- Get rid of your annual long-distance service fee, and only use an access code when you dial, which is rare and cheap anyway.
- Decide which satellite channels you can do without and offer up a couple of shows that you really enjoy. On your monthly bill, you can save more than $20.00.
- Check the reduced-for-quick-sale carts and racks first when you buy fruits, fruit, and bread at the grocery store.
- Adjust the oil of your own cars.
- Save money at the end of the season / during the offseason while ordering clothing for the next year. You will get fantastic deals down to the mark.
- Take the spare change from your pockets every evening or regularly clean your purse and set the coins aside. Never take back some capital before the year's end. Take all the coins to the bank, then swap them for currency. You'll be shocked to find out that they added up to $50, $100, or even $200.
- "Take care of the cents, and then take care of your dollars."
- cycle, instead of commuting to save on petrol, to work in decent conditions.
- Eat a few hearty meals per week for vegetarians.
- For a fantastic source of kitchen goods, books, clothes, and furniture, visit yard sales.
- Do not purchase bottled water! Purchase a decent filter for water, and drink tap water.
- Put all your changes into an empty coffee can at the end of each day. And when you watch TV or listen to the radio, roll coins. This can really easily add up to hundreds of dollars and give you something good to do to relax with your hands.

Saving money by lowering the cost of your energy. Power, along with the cost of rent or mortgage and food, maybe the number two or three expenses.

Switch any single bulb to fluorescent compact bulbs. They can be pricey, but they last for years (no more replacements) and appear to use only 10-20% of the standard bulbs' capacity. Buy one any time you make a shopping trip, starting with the kitchen or stairway in the heavy traffic areas of the house until you no longer have any incandescent bulbs left.

Consider converting all-electric heating equipment to natural gas, such as the hot water heater, refrigerator, stove, or dryer, if you own your house. For practically any unit, electricity can be used and for that, you pay a hefty electricity premium. For heating systems, gas is very effective; it heats up far faster and wastes much less electricity.

In cold water, do all of your laundries. In cold weather, most contemporary detergents are just as successful as in hot water. Often, make sure that whatever laundry you do is a full and total load - it takes the same amount of energy as a tenth of a load.

Try this trick on your dryer: put it on for 20 minutes, then put it on for 15 minutes with "air fluff." With the water coming off as steam, your clothes are now heated and you'll find that while it takes only 20 minutes longer, you save about 50 percent of your dryer's energy costs.

Switch the heat up to your ideal temperature during the winter months anytime you need to use your furnace. Turn the thermostat to the off spot when the furnace shuts off (your house has been heated up to temperature). Test the thermostat if you feel cold. Switch the thermostat back up to your ideal temperature if you're 5 degrees below your desired temperature.

Furnaces can always kick in and out to sustain the correct temperature, but while they are in the heat cycle for longer periods, furnaces are much more efficient. You're going to save over 50 percent on the cost of your heater, and even 30 percent on a high-tech wireless thermostat. Keep it off absolutely, of course, while you're out of the building.

Unplug all if you do leave the house for the weekend or longer. The flashing alarm clock or VCR or DVD on standby always needs control. When you leave the house for a week you will save real money by actually unplugging all these gadgets, and if there is a breakdown or power surge, you will shield your home from fire hazards.

Keep your freezer and fridge as full as you can. The less the storage area in your fridge, the less time it takes to cool the air in your fridge or freezer. Don't you have a lot of cash for food? Only buy a lot of bread and chuck it in the fridge. If you buy it in big amounts anyway, you will typically find bread cheaper.

If you just need a magazine subscription, a small party could be made up of three individuals to share the costs. Then, for one week each person will keep the magazine.

By tossing away any catalogs or magazines that tempt you to buy more, you save money.

It is easy to ice cereal and preserves it for a very long time. We could never eat it soon enough before that and had to throw it out because it was stale. You will never know it was frozen until you spilled milk on it. I haven't seen any cereal that tasted bad in the freezer yet.

Don't throw your empty milk bags out. Break them open and wash them instead. As baggies, you should have them. When used as a sealer, they also hold frozen foods healthy.

Save money by making meals for the next week by making your shopping list and buying just what is on your list.

Instead of renting, borrow DVDs from your friends and family.

Set your washer to the shortest possible wash configuration. Put it on for 5 minutes instead of cleaning the clothing for 10 minutes. This saves wear and tear on your electric bill and on your clothing.

On the streets or in parking lots, sweep up the pennies, dimes, and nickels found. Add money to the pot of spare change you are collecting and you can add all cash to the emergency fund before the end of the year.

Promote the practice of team sports among your children. The more time you spend playing sports with your children, the less time and money they can spend in the shopping mall.

Do not load the gas tank to the brim to save money on diesel, as the additional weight of the fuel takes an extra toll on the engine capacity. Take out all things in the trunk that are not necessary for vehicle weight reduction.

Look at other people's budget-conscious films. Purchase your own popcorn jar and add some seasonings of your own.

Switch off the sun at night and use a hot water bottle to sleep. In a tiny apartment, this works well because it easily heats up. Turning the heat off could fit well too, for those with bigger homes.

Espresso sounds like a luxurious option if you have to drink a specialty coffee, but since its ground thinner, and you consume less the coffee lasts longer.

Check for items such as razors, lotions, computer applications, baby food, diapers, etc. on eBay You'll save if you can think ahead.

Each pay cycle set aside every amount on which you had budgeted but did not have to spend. You may have expected, for example, that $50 might be required to maintain your vehicle, but you just had to pay $30. Take the $20 "extra" and put it in the bank account.

Quite possibly YOU can save while on a shoestring

Believe it or not, how much you save has nothing to do with how many you earn and this has been shown by research! It's time for reasons to be set away; here's a guide for finding money that you didn't even realize you had.

Which One Simple Word - Savings

Do you feel a profound sense of remorse when you hear that single, easy word? You do of course-we all do. That is because 75 percent of respondents said they recognized that their investments, intended for retirement, were inadequate, like most Americans.

Perhaps this is a source of anxiety, but not even as remarkable as the realization that how much you invest now has absolutely little to do with how affluent you are now. In fact, this is so true that the middle-income earners in the same study managed to save less than the lower-income earners. Now when you think about it it's remarkable. Those with more saved fewer! What is the secret to their success in savings?

These numbers are both disturbing and humiliating for those of us who scrimp and invest relentlessly and have too little to show for it! It also means that you have no reason for investments that are insufficient.

The bottom line here is this: you just have to save, no matter what! That means you MUST sock away at least $1 in savings for every $10 you earn. Doesn't sound that rough, doesn't it? FALSE!

You cannot save a single red cent because you have an iron-clad savings scheme! The trick lies in the intent and the strategy!

What's your EMERGENCY PLAN?

Isn't it time TO START A very good SAVINGS PLAN?

You are willing, but as to how you can come up with the extra money, you feel at a loss. You're just eking out life now. When you teach yourself to behave differently, you can do it. The first part of any good idea is that. You've got to think properly. If you don't care about your finances right now, you won't be able to handle it.

Your First Step: Think again about how you think about money

Saving money is a state of mind that is calm. You have to say NO to all the spending before you can even proceed, and stop pretending that you really need all the things you waste all of your hard-earned money on. Don't just invest.

That's clear enough! Say NO to all the excuses and explanations that you felt you MUST be investing. Say yourself, PERIOD, No More Excuses! Take the $50 or $100 out of your pockets the very next time you want to buy something rather than stash it hidden elsewhere. Are you seeing logic? That is why you're naming it preserving. You're not ending up with things; you are ending up with hard-earned dollars.

Thinking of frugality as the savior would be another new way of thinking. Become a cheapskate confirmed and do what your most frugal mates do. Take careful note of the fact that rather than buying a new one, frugal friends patch the shower curtain. Sit down with families of the Depression-era and inquire if, through even hopeless periods, they made ends meet. To economize, you want to read.

In rethinking, the next step is to become empowered. Spend all your free time online to discover some pages that are frugal. "You'll find a ton of good websites dedicated to living on less, such as thefrugalshopper.com, simpleliving.net, and frugaliving.com. Take a look at "living cheaply," "frugal living" and "voluntary simplicity.

Learn to turn time for shopping into time for activity. Go on a bike ride, take the kids to the beach, stroll down memory lane, do something and everything you can to take your mind off shopping and saving. It's functioning!

Step #2: Time for Investments!

There are a lot of innovative ways to survive for fewer. You do not want to make your life boring, however. Here are a few fantastic ways to save money without losing the quality of life.

Don't worry about it so much—just do it! Direct deposit is your best buddy right now! In your IRA, 401(k), or money market portfolio, your money is whisked away, and you don't have to do anything to make that so. Only drop and fill out the forms through your payroll department and/or your bank. Today do so.

Feed meatless meat for a bit. Hey, go veggie. Get ready for only three meatless days a week without replacing costly fish) and you can save $25 a week which is $100 a month, which is $1,200 a year! Beans: You're going to learn to enjoy them.

Play a game with money. Set it back for later if you get a $5 bill. Instead, do the same with others with neighborhoods, or sometimes all your spare change. Before you ever lose a nickel, you'll have a nest egg set up.

Don't ever waste any extras. Save both the income-tax rebate, the people's holiday capital, the telephone company's $20.38 overpayment audit, and any other extras and save every cent.

Haggle and Bargain. You will be impressed that airlines, restaurants, credit card providers, and even computer/appliance/rug salespeople will drop their costs, fees, and interest rates. Haggle a little first, before you even think about paying the full price.

Re-assess the cash before you spend it. The family dinner is going to cost more than you spent in a week on food. Half the cost of a commuter pass is worth that fancy pair of trainers. Learn what your money is worth to you and you're not going to be able to dispose of it that easily.

Don't overpay the taxes now. Yeah, you enjoy having a big refund every spring from the IRS. However, the irony is that you are basically lending money to the government and are interest-free. Go over your tax return to see how you can hang on and maybe get a $150 rebate until Dec. 31. If you use it for an emergency, and bank the payout when you get it later, you can spend the money NOW that way.

Decide to increase the deductibles on the policies. For the different kinds of insurance, reassess each of the deductibles. Your rates will decrease if you can increase them at all.

Reduce interest payments. Check whether the pace is too high or not. If it is, look at refinancing, which will save you cash. Now, let's have a peek at the private mortgage insurance (PMI) you paid when you didn't have enough cash to make a down payment of 20 percent. Be sure that it is canceled if the equity of your house is higher than 22 percent. The rule is that. Lastly, pay down your debt. If you can afford an additional $100 a month, over the long term, you can save thousands of interest payments.

Toss the ugly, shiny catalogs back. Catalogs are the best-known type of spending temptation known to man or woman. They are sure to be fun and look fine, but are they worth the spending risk? Chuck them into the bin, right out.

Withhold such excessive payments. Like the $2.50 you spend only because the ATM is right there as opposed to going two miles to the bank right now, where any time you use your cash card, you don't get paid at all. As an option, how about the late payments for video returns? These truly add up. Don't forget the banks hit you with those fat charges when you write a check that, yeah, bounces.

Yourself, vacuum it. "I discovered a really cool trick: I wash it when a clothing label says, "Dry Clean Only, On the other side, using an old-fashioned washing method cleverly referred to as a sponge, dab off the little mustard spot.

Yeah, don't hire a pro. If you can repair the garage door for the neighbor and she can paint the kitchen: go and save it.

Place the boost in your bank. Place your direct deposit on the modest 3 percent to 5 percent increase in the paycheck and survive on your former wage.

For long-distance, pay wise. Test for worth any of the multiple telecommunications plans. Pay heed to what you are spending every minute now. You could be offered a better rate by certain dial-around codes or inexpensive calling cards (one without a surcharge per call). Not only are you able to save, but you will even realize you don't need to chat too much to Alvin in Schenectady.

Only purchase the basics for your dogs. To pet pampering, say no. Will, your dog needs some cookies with the t-bone? Does that rabbit-fur-lined toy need your cat? Probably not.

A promise never to pay the full price again. Hop on to the World Wide Web the next time you need to browse. For exceptional suppliers of "lightly used" items, from books to jewelry to office furniture, search for eBay, half.com, and craigslist.org, including the entire first season of Star Trek on camera.

When you are concentrating on investing, you worry about improvements in money. You've had big savings before you know it.

Smart Tips for Living on a Budget

No matter what the current patterns are, regardless of the moment of history and no matter what the current state of the economy, no matter what the unemployment rate is or where interest rates are certain money-saving solutions still succeed and remain real.

Significant improvements come from little measures and you will see a big change in your life if you plan to bring any one of these many savings secrets into effect.

Now you can discover a range of tips for savings. In a number of down-to-earth ways, you can learn how to better put your hard-earned cash. What you'll learn in your day-to-day life will set you up beautifully.

Tip 1 on Money Saving:

The great Albert Einstein once said, "To see the obvious requires a genius."

Let you be guided today by these wise words. What he means by that is that the simpler stuff in life is the most powerful often... But we prefer to ignore them because they are so simple, and we don't make them work for us.

One of the most important ideas for money-making is this: keep a daily diary of all you spend. Go to the dollar store, buy a little book, and take it everywhere you go with you. Write down every penny you spend—every single penny. It is just as convenient as that.

If you do one thing, after just a few weeks, you can realize that something magical is happening in your financial life.

In writing down each of the expenses, there is something extremely powerful. It makes it more practical and exacting the flow of money through your life. It tells you exactly where you are investing your money, on what, and why simply and clearly. When you know this, managing your spending becomes even easier. With self-control, you will feel motivated and this will promote saving.

Not only have many people who have taken up this profession learned much about themselves that they had never known before, but they are also surprised at the simplicity of the lesson learned.

For example, by analyzing their notebook, a person might discover that they have actually spent almost $1,000 on diet soft drinks, snacks, and candy bars over the year! Since their work only takes in $20,000 a year, they found that something completely trivial was frittering away 5 percent of their entire profits. The individual gave up the snacks and beverages and noticed out the next year they had enough money to go on holiday. Which one would you prefer if you had the option between snacks and a much-needed vacation? Of course, you'd pick a weekend, all of us would.

The point is it was their daily spending record that helped to achieve the perspective and transparency they needed to monitor their finances. That's what a clear budget log is going to do for you - it's going to give you much-needed leverage of your expenditure, and thus your financial life. Between your life of financial hardship and financial independence, there may be nothing but a 75-cent notebook and a ballpoint pen.

Tip 2 on Money Saving:

Avoid wasting on deficits! We also understand how Uncle Sam generated debt, investing more money than our nation took in. It's called spending on the deficit. Well, don't do the same thing! For you and me, the same rules exist. The "American Way" may be using those nasty little credit cards, but it's a debt-making way that any new day produces lots of fools.

The typical credit card holder is holding nearly $8,000 in plastic debt today!

It's definitely very easy to spend on this sort of credit card debt, which many of you may know. The explanation is mental. It's just not the same as turning over a stack of green dollar bills when you send the clerk a credit card. Will you fork over a pocketful of $10 bills as quickly as throwing a credit card over a counter? Probably not. For most, this one is a no-brainer!

Credit cards are dragging you into debt and keeping you there. Even for those with decent wages, it can be extremely hard to pay off your credit card balance to zero. Moreover, make no bones about it; credit card debt will drain your financial vitality just as quickly as your physical body will be drained by an exposed vein in its own life energy. Using a credit card by preference will easily change to using it if necessary. You are still in trouble whenever you get to that point, and it is time to get some help.

Also, tiny installments will gradually add up until you stop contributing to the debt. When you are diligent and self-disciplined, you will get out of debt. If the cards are history, a stringent pay-as-you-go scheme must be implemented. Save now and shop when you have the entire cost, instead of spending now and paying later. It's necessary to be able to save.

Once again, one of the most important financial resources open to us today is to avoid credit-oriented consumption. Why not use this tool to pick it up for yourself?

Tip 3 on Money Saving:

Just sell all your garbage. That's right; the time for a serious yard sale is long gone. Check for any single thing you don't really need in your house or apartment, and then sell it all! Every final item!

Grab an inventory. The fact is most individuals are shocked by what they own - just how much money they have wrapped up with things they no longer need and use. Why let it just sit down and accumulate dust while in a savings account it might gather interest instead?

You could quickly get $600, $1,200, $1,200,... At the end of the week, also $5,000 is richer. You'd get your spot washed up as an extra bonus, and you'd have a new sense of starting all over again. A garage sale is an exceptional place to proceed. Not only can you clean your home, but it often also provides a social lift that lets people keep their lives and finances under control.

Tip 4 on Money Saving:

Long ago, Ben Franklin said A penny saved is a penny earned." Yeah, it's still accurate and still one of the most important tips in the history of moneymaking.

The challenge of saving is well known in Franklin's famous remark.

It's hard to invest and much better to waste! That we all remember! That's why because it takes so much work to hang on to that currency, every penny saved is really won! It can work magic in your life if you can do it. It would de-stress your life to get a savings account. Imagine getting ahead of, rather than behind, your bills. When you are in front of your expenses, all of your life is within your own hands. At night, you sleep better. Your mind is more open to coming up with new ways of making and spending more money. Saving is infectious - until you let it begin!

Some suggestions to help you save:

1. Don't settle for proof of interest. Get a different bank account that can't be opened as readily as a checking account.
2. Hold your money in another branch, one that's off the normal road, or maybe in another area. That way, each time you visit the bank to make a checking deposit, you would not be tempted to tap into it.
3. Invest in short-term savings bonds that have maturity periods of 6 months to one year. In case of real money crises, you'll get a higher cost, while holding your money tight at the same time.
4. Open the account with two separate names, if you may, and need all signatures to make a withdrawal. Every withdrawal may be discussed by two individuals to hold each other in line.
5. Place a minimum of 5 percent automatically in your bank account as you get your paycheck. You will be shocked by how much you have really saved in only a year, and you will feel fantastic about it.

Visualize daily prosperity and resources. Am I honestly saying that you are following a kind of mysticism that makes you a "money magnet"? Perhaps yes, perhaps no. Name it what you want-a a mind game, mysticism, Modern Age-the strong truth is that a good mentality towards money is behind any rich man and woman.

Look at it like this: getting either negative or positive feelings costs Nothing one way or the other. Then why not think confidently AND lift the ODDS?

Many experiments have been performed on the habits of thought and the mentality of some of the world's wealthiest, most influential individuals. An optimistic outlook towards money and their desire to gain and retain it was the one thing that they both had in common.

WHAT HAVE YOU LEARNED?

RESPECT MONEY AND THINK POSITIVELY TOWARDS MONEY. THIS IS A FANTASTIC START TO MEANINGFUL SAVINGS.

In the first place, the trick to being able to collect emergency funds when needed most is to be in the proper frame of mind about money. Think of cash and saving favorably, and conserve. That equation you can't beat!

Seven Serious Ways to Cut costs - Not for the Faint of Heart

Are you still interested in saving? Take a serious look at how you invest and change it afterward. Take a roommate, park your car, and you'll save as much as $10,000 a year. Stop smoking those cigars. It's always just as easy as all that!

Are you finding it harder and harder to blame your measly paycheck for savings shortfalls?

Will it surprise you to hear that your salary has nothing to do with how much you are saving? Well, it is, in truth, quite real. If you want to invest and are able to change your investments to raise your savings has much to do with it.

A new analysis by Venti and Wise, "Choice, Chance and Wealth Dispersion at Retirement," showed a very large spectrum of how many individuals were willing to prepare for retirement at the same income levels. It was not just the higher-income individuals who managed to save the most the report pointed out. Indeed, even persons in the lowest wage classes have been able to save as much as $100,000 more than any of their middle-income counterparts.

What did their inference come to? On the verge of retirement, individuals with no savings have actually decided not to invest as much and spend more over their lifetimes.

So the key is very simple: spend less than you earn and SAVE Money.

Why any individuals get into financial trouble is plain to see.

Some people don't pause to realize that only one aspect of the financial well-being equation is making money. Learning how to spend money and invest in the other important component.

For too many, a major part of the issue is that individuals simply don't know enough about their own financial facts. They don't know what they earn, they don't know what it takes to live comfortably, and they don't know their actual, disposable money, either.

What could be the answer?

Individuals have to know themselves. Sit back and find out the actual sales and performance through your monthly bills and statements. Then, decide if what you see is what you want. If not, create a concrete strategy to improve that.

Ask yourself these four important questions to assist with the process:

What is my actual and present financial picture?

- ❖ Why will I like to live?
- ❖ Can this be funded by my actual money, and how do I really want to use my money?
- ❖ How do I make the most use of my money?

Treat your money to be handled like every other household chore and devote enough time each month to handle it.

Notice that Many of the financial devices that have made life more comfortable, such as credit cards, will facilitate very poor financial behavior and when misused, prolong debt. Credit cards can be used strictly as the instrument of cash control that they are and not as a vehicle for borrowing.

Bear in mind that anytime you place stuff on a credit card, you use tomorrow's money. Bit by bit, you keep shutting yourself up and losing your rights.

The important thing on health that is fiscal is Stop Spending

Much more Serious Savings Strategies

You would want to curtail the buyer in you if you are adamant about getting a balanced emergency money fund. This means investing instead of spending. Of note, getting a part of your weekly paycheck immediately deposited to your bank account remains the number one, easiest form of investing. If you like the thought of determining how much savings you are going to deposit, take heart, and change a serious tip or two, week by week. It's all fine if better and more savings are the end product.

Keep, once and for all, the "mother" to all garage sales! Do your homework and do the inventory of a house practically. Journey down to the furthest reach of any wardrobe, all the way back, and determine that it would have to go if you haven't used it for more than six months. Many persons have yard sale pieces tucked away in their homes worth at least $1,000. For several, it turns out to be a veritable gold mine.

Only how badly do you need the ugly, pack-a-day habit of smoking? That's potentially $5 a day in Washington state or around $1,800 a year which will go straight into your savings. The benefits in premiums and health care may not even begin to touch it.

Tame the driving tiger that is inside you. Carpool or use public transit instead. This will save you, not to mention the money wasted on a cough, on petrol, premiums and repair expenses. You could save $1,141 a year by traveling half the time for 50 weeks of the year (based on a 25-mile roundtrip commute) using the IRS' 2002 mileage reimbursement rate of 36.5 cents a mile as a metric for the expense of commuting. If you work in the area, imagine nixing your vehicle for a much more serious solution. Any cities are also introducing advanced systems that allow you to get access to a vehicle without ownership problems (such as "Flexcar" in Seattle, Portland, and Washington, D.C.) without ownership problems.

Purchase used objects. According to the U.S., the average customer spends around $1,750 a year on clothes and maintenance. The most recent Consumer Spending Report by the Office of Labour Statistics. By shopping at consignment stores and auctions, you can quickly cut it in half, while the life of the items might be a little shorter than purchasing new ones. The annual savings can only amount to 25 percent or $437 to pay for it.

Only being a homebody. On average, entertainment consumption has a way of chewing away from the best-planned budgets, at just over $1,800 a year. For books, music, and film, imagine the library. Eat less often out. The average person spends $2,276 on dining out a year. For annual savings of more than $1,900, consider cutting your spending in half in both regions.

Split the spending on housing. Although some cash can be saved with a transfer around the lines, transfers are costly. Try getting a room leased out in your building. The estimated per-person housing costs were just over $13,200 in 2004. Rooms quickly go for $400 a month in metropolitan regions like Seattle. Around $20 of the figure goes to raises in utility rates, even before any payroll taxes, you've already realized annual savings of more than $4,000.

Cut all of the credit cards. Next, create an emergency fund to handle the most unforeseen costs. This helps you to become a banking entity on your own. Credit cards may be a management mechanism for cash flow, but for years, spending just the minimum would trap you in debt.

According to market study company CardWeb.com, if you're the average American with at least one credit card, you currently have up to $8,523 in credit card debt. With an annual APR of 14.4 percent, interest rates alone could cost you as much as $1,100 a year. You might eliminate such interest charges by merely waiting until you've saved enough money to make transactions.

You might be staring at savings of about $12,000 a year if you're very ambitious and follow all the above advice. Figuring that the investments continue to accumulate beautifully and quickly at the historical rate of return of 10 percent. Go for the emergency fund rather than the mortgage, and invest.

Make Small Cuts for Savings that are Huge

In your favor, tip the wheel of generating money. Naturally, one way is to pay less. Nevertheless to make sure the money works better for you, set targets to guarantee that it does.

Many have asked what a foolproof way of producing wealth would be. Is it to buy top-paying stocks on the Internet or work with a tech startup that provides you with lucrative stock options? Is the trick of counting every penny or is the path to riches risk-paved? Will you need to be especially clever and well-connected? Is being rich, alternatively, a question of luck?

The response is there is no one, a real path to riches, and for more than only a few famous persons, both of the above have produced wealth. However, by following a couple of basic precepts, you will place the chances of generating wealth on your side.

1. Spend less than what you're making.

This may be the most misunderstood case when many people think it's a matter of scaling down on their present level of life, a tactic for many people that is much too complicated. Yeah, by spending less money dining out or getting fun out you will influence your personal balance sheet. It would make a slight change in the cash flow to make a cup of coffee at the office instead of getting a $3 espresso. However, the greatest change would be made on the sales side of the ledger.

If you want to be on the right route to investing, stop looking at your budget like a pie that has to be broken into bits of different sizes. Instead, think about how you can increase the size of the pie by attempting to work out how the multiple pieces will cover your expenses. Yes, you might apply for a boost from your manager. Find out at the same time if you can start making more cash on the side. Start dreaming about how the current pie will sweeten you.

Care of how you spend your time and your money as well. Perhaps you will earn an additional $80 by being a waiter or bartender instead of taking the family out this weekend. You could serve as a salesclerk to raise some spare cash instead of taking the kids shopping at the mall.

If you don't want to work every weekend, start by dreaming about working every other weekend. Taking charge of a few other kids on Saturday or Sunday instead of paying for a baby sitter when you enjoy a gig, allowing busy parents to run their errands. When it comes to working on the holiday, make a move. Time and money will spare you this.

Then you should save it so that the money can work for you instead of wasting the additional money you receive from your part-time work. You will come to enjoy your spare time so much better as you do this.

2. Make it work for you with your money.

Having your money do the job is the ultimate key to financial success, so you can rest. This calls for ample investment dollars to be accrued so that growth and profits will release you from the need to work any harder. Punching a time clock is the last thing you'll like to do.

Some extremely affluent individuals choose to operate simply because they love what they do so much. They are also redefining work to involve the management of their assets. For the rich, all of them will go hand in hand.

You'll hear wherever you go, "I never get to the point where I don't have to go back to work because I can't afford to set aside money today." The influence of compound interest is underestimated by these individuals.

Any employee with earned income is now entitled to open a non-deductible IRA or, better still, a Roth IRA. The annual donation of $3,000 a year averages out at a weekly expense of $57.69. Every hard-working American can achieve this objective.

In comparison, in 30 years, a $3,000 annual investment in a Roth IRA, rising tax-free at the historical 10.6 percent rate for the capital market, rises to more than $500,000. According to the MSN Money Savings Calculator, if you start in your twenties and put $3,000 in the same Roth IRA every year, at 10.6 percent, you will have a nest egg of about $5.2 million at age 70. And with an annual return of 8 percent, you would end up with $1.9 million.

3. Make confident that your money works for you, rather than against you.

If you make the correct decisions and follow a strategy of daily spending, your capital will work really powerfully for you. Around the same time, deep potholes would be put on your path to prosperity by inaccurate money decisions.

Credit-card debt is a classic example. Consider the case of a customer who spends $2,000 at 19.8 percent interest and a $40 monthly fee on a credit card. It would take you 31 years and two months to pay off the debt if you make just the minimum monthly contributions (and many individuals do only that)! In comparison, you'll pocket an extra $8,202 in financing costs along the way. That logic is ridiculous!

What would be so important to change now that it places you in debt for a much longer time than it is possible that the item will last? (Of course, a mortgage lasts 30 years, so during that span, the debt is deductible and the house can rise in value.) Most of the things you choose to charge on your card have a much shorter life. For several, they can do without a particular transaction altogether.

If you're still in debt, you could get out of debt in less than three years if you only double the minimum monthly contribution. The smartest way to move on the journey to financial liberty is to pay off existing debt.

4. Hold your wallet with a secure clasp

You'll note several deductions when you take a quick glance at your paycheck before you get to the sum that you can cash or put in the savings. There are definitely exemptions for Social Security, federal, and maybe state taxes on wages.

That's the money that comes out of your paycheck before you even get the ability to make choices about it. Money set aside for the creation of wealth should be handled in the very same way. Be sure you sign up for the highest possible payout if your employer has a 401(k) retirement account. Each pay cycle will immediately be taken out of your paycheck. (And if all or part of your donation is matched by your company, failing to sign up is like walking away from free money!)

If you have no hope of compulsory deductions for a retirement account for a company or even a U.S. Payroll deduction scheme for savings bonds, and you'll have to build your own automated savings plan. Ask if the employer will automatically deposit your paycheck into your bank account or pledge to do so yourself the day you collect the check.

Then to make daily deposits into an IRA, sign up with a mutual fund provider for an automatic monthly deduction scheme. You can also automatically set up a deduction for the U.S. On the website, Savings Bonds. The entire point of this is to get the money as soon as possible out of your bank account before you see it and use it.

5. Establish savings and spending targets for capital.

Around the age of 40 or 50 or by the time you retire, would you like to have $1 million? You certainly can!

Start by setting targets on your own. Never set a target that you are not able to control. Your ambitions should not depend on your employer giving you a raise; your own actions must be attainable. By gaining further schooling or preparation, you might need to invest in yourself so you can apply for a career that pays more.

By taking on a second position that pays fees instead of a set wage, you might need to take more risk in your finances or in your lifestyle. Assess the risks involved, and realize that you will get a bigger return by having the odds on your side.

Emergency Money Strategy while Coping with Debt, Financial Family and Stress

Due to lost employment, divorce, death in the family, or being overrun by debt, etc., financial stress is usual among those pushed into frugality. This can lead an individual to feel nervous, terrified, anxious, irritated, and of course, depressed.

These same emotions are easily the number one source of bad decisions on money management. These bad choices will lead to unmanageable loads of debt which will launch a vicious panic spiral that never appears to stop.

Your feelings of helplessness will become so debilitating as you hit this stage, and you find yourself in a money emergency, that you simply stop working in the real world.

YOU Have TO HAVE your WITS ABOUT RAISING EMERGENCY MONEY

Get yourself Immediate Help

Get the support you need right away if you notice any of the above qualities of yourself. Seek out a licensed psychiatrist... Speak to a friend or member of your family... but talk to someone! If you meet someone who demonstrates the characteristics above, try to help them! If you lend cash, an ear, give some helpful advice or help them get advice, do something doesn't matter.

The first thing you need to understand is that there is no hopeless situation. You can do what it takes to get out of desperate situations with only a little encouragement and persistence, along with a couple of well thought out ambitions, and moral support from family and friends.

A new outlook, new talent, and most of all, a new sense of self-esteem can be changed. Do not encourage someone to convince you otherwise and if they do, lock the same door they entered and do not open it again! To help you get to the other side, all you need is positive reinforcement and not negativity.

Seek out your True Friends

It typically does not take too long for you to know who actually cares about you, who is genuinely a friend when you are struggling to collect emergency funds. If they're family or not. In your time of need, your friends will be there for you, give support, and lend an ear so that you can just speak. Speak for guidance in coming up with positive ideas about how during such a tough period in your life you might collect emergency funds. Be open to the many ideas that will be offered to you.

Get ready to Set the Priorities

The time comes when you need to set your emotions aside and just reflect on your well-being and your family. During periods of financial hardship and upheaval, this needs to be your priority. In periods of financial hardship, if you can't cope as a mom or dad, how can you expect your kids to cope now or in the future? To derive inspiration from them, you must set a precedent for the rest of the family.

So make the decision today to learn how to cope, make the adjustments you can, remain centered and goal-oriented, and let fear and financial stress go out the door so that you are prepared to deal with any cash crises that come your way.

You have to have the ability to come up with a few quick cash fixes (with no more borrowing) to recuperate from a cash Emergency:

Budgeting tip #1: To get back on track really fast, the first thing you want to do is focus. If that means letting a little bit of your credit card balance go, so be it. Call the credit card issuers to order lowered interest rates and fees as soon as you know that you have a money emergency. Not just one, but both!

Budgeting Tip #2: Contact the creditor for your auto loan to offer a payment extension. Maybe you dislike payment extensions because they require a premium because, at the completion of the deal, you will have to make the payment. In this scenario, an extension of payment will allow a little breathing space to help you heal during your cash emergency. For the expansion, assume that you would possibly have to pay a premium (usually around 1/4 - 1/3 of the amount of the car payment). At this point, freeing up the money you need today is your first and only priority.

Budgeting tip #3: Check to see whether, for a nominal fee, the mortgage holder would approve an extension. Today, do this!

Budgeting Tip #4: Hosting an on-the-spot yard sale is another fast remedy. There's not so much time for you to prepare, so do a short survey of your personal belongings. Come up with things that no longer fit, but are in decent shape, as well as things you bought but no longer use, knick-knacks, plates, and books. Throw all together, fast. At laundry mats and grocery stores across town, put some notices up on the same day, and remember to add a sign at the end of your driveway. With so little time and effort, you can make a fast $300 this way.

Budgeting Tip #5: If you have a bigger thing to sell, contact the local radio stations to see if on weekends they have a "call-in swap show." This is a very common way to turn mildly used and more costly products to fast cash easily.

Budgeting tip #6: With utility and telecommunications bills, another fast choice is. Request that the existing bill (plus any past debt you owe) be set aside with a budget plan if you are not currently on a budget plan. Expect a down payment (usually 1/4 of the bill) to be charged and that all subsequent bills (while on the spending schedule for the back payment) must be kept current. The nice thing about it the nice thing... Usually, it's interest-free, and for a month, it will give you some much-needed breathing room. However, you must be confident that in the coming month, you will retain the daily energy expenses AND the budget payments.

Budget tip #7: Consult with the family church for emergency assistance. One of the best ways to find out what is needed in the neighborhood to support people in need or in times of disaster may be local churches. Test, first with the local church.

Getting Fast Cash through Borrowing

Having Easy Cash by Borrowing

If you are in a true cash emergency, completely, definitely, in a bind, and you've tried all of the above, so try borrowing. Ask your family first then your nearest bank.

As a last resort, you might want to try what's known as a "Payday Loan." If anything else fails, certain types of borrowing stores may be helpful.

A Few Timely Lessons in Simple Living

It needs a lot of forethought to prepare for a fiscal emergency. Rather than having to struggle to come up with the cash when the need is highest, it is best to start saving now.

- ❖ Adapt any strategic thinking.
- ❖ Reprogram your mind to become a saver right now.
- ❖ Easy living outcomes with only millions in savings
- ❖ Remind yourself you can do less than
- ❖ Make a deliberate decision to survive with the sun.
- ❖ Place the whole family on a budget
- ❖ Discuss techniques for how to build the first budget

Better Money Management Thinking

When it comes to how we spend our money or time, the first step to making healthier decisions is living and behaving deliberately and questioning everyday money and job patterns.

Simple living is primarily about making healthier life choices: about how we invest, eat, develop society, and spend our spare time.

It's NOT necessarily less to eat. Smarter OR is to be eaten differently.

When it comes to consumption, we do NOT only blindly go ahead.

Just say no to the purchasing compulsion,

- Put it down if you see something you like and dream about it for at least a few days. Chances are the instinct has to leave.
- A look at other entertainment outlets
- Find opportunities to socialize and build your own entertainment that does not revolve around pricey tabs for restaurants or tickets for events.
- Dedicate time to quiet time
- Quiet time encourages you to refresh your spiritual battery and gives you the time you need to think about life and make better decisions.
- Know that after all, time is money.
- This problem of time is going to loom much bigger than money. We have assumed, as a society, that time is capital. Both are closely related. Spend time prudently.

Each day Money Saving Tips

How you can Cut costs on Gas

Gas rates just keep going up, and the scale of our pockets keeps shrinking. This how-to will show you at the nearby gas station more tips to save money.

Measures

1. Get a credit card taken away. When you use the card for transactions, certain credit cards give petrol savings. It operates in about the same manner as, when you use your card for sales, certain credit card providers grant you frequent flyer miles.
2. Get a membership card for petrol. Seek benefits from membership. Moreover, when you use their supermarket membership cards, department and grocery stores offer discounts at the gasoline pump. It is possible (at the time of this writing) to fill a car's tank for .79 cents a gallon by shopping at the Giant Eagle grocery store and using their membership card, with savings of $1.36 per gallon.
3. Give a decent tuning up for your car. Although offering a tune-up to your car won't really save you money at the pump, it's going to save you petrol. Overall, consuming less petrol saves you money. Get the oil checked, and give the engine a double over from a professional mechanic.
4. For sales, visit the WWW. Web pages let you explore the best offers in your area.
5. Purchase an electric vehicle. Not only do electric vehicles earn you instant pump savings, but tax breaks are also provided by the U.S. government and your local state to persons who use gas-saving cars. Federal deductions can be as high as $2000 for using vehicles that conserve petrol. Try buying a normal car with a decent MPG (miles per gallon), like the Toyota Echo, if you can't afford the increasing number of electric cars out there.
6. Switch the AC off. Running the car's air conditioning places more pressure on the engine of the car. This leads to the car consuming more petrol per mile. Save fuel, use less petrol. Depending on the car you drive, the AC could put less drag on your car at highway speeds than if all the windows are open. You may however want to keep it calm on the highway.
7. Using the cheaper stuff. Many new vehicles run almost as well on cheap petrol as on more costly gas. In reality, engineers believe

that the car buyer would use cheap petrol, and so the engine of the car is built accordingly.
8. When rates are bigger, don't fill the tank. Gas producers and operators of gas stations will charge high gas rates when they know that customers are going to pay for it. The owners watch how much gas people put in their vehicles each day. This shows the owners that customers are going to pay the high cost if they increase the price a few cents and people are already filling up their tanks. When rates are high, adding just a few gallons to the vehicle sends a message to the owners that customers aren't pleased with the high prices.
9. Drive, don't. Don't drive while you certainly don't have to. Not only can you save cash by carpooling, cycling, taking the bus, and riding a bike, but they are safer for the environment and could be better for your wellbeing. When it's just a few blocks down the highway, do you really need to drive to the store?
10. Check the air pressure of the tyres weekly. Buy an affordable electric air pump (not a pencil gauge as they are not reliable) and an accurate tire gauge. Keep both tyres filled at the same pressure, but not your tire, as suggested for your vehicle. Go by the doorframe sticker and not the tyre wall.
11. Drive at a slow pace and keep the windows closed. The drag on your vehicle is minimized by having the windows locked. Also, keeping to the speed limit helps. Thus it uses fewer gear shifts and fewer engine revolutions. Stop accelerating quickly, or unexpectedly braking. When you can, use cruise control.
12. In your car, clear out any unused things. Delete them if you have bulky items in your vehicle that you do not use. If your car is lighter, less gasoline can be needed to drive you to where you are going.
13. Stop leaving the engine idle. You will save petrol by shutting the car off and restarting when you are ready to drive if you are going to be stuck for longer than one minute.
14. On cold days, purchase. On cool days, buy petrol and, if you can, drive on hot days. You buy more "mass" petrol for the same price when you buy on cold days and pay for the amount. Never fill the tank full or as it gets colder, it can leak.

Simpler Solutions for Managing your Money

Let's face it it takes a little more innovative thinking to come up with clever and easy ways to save money.

To control the finances, use certain of these shortcuts. It is assumed that they will save you time and money.

Cheat your mind to save

Can't you really find out where your money is going? There is an easy solution: to waste less and save more by tricking your own mind.

If you're up for a challenge, grant a weekly allowance to yourself. Put a fixed amount of allowance into an envelope and decide that for every given week this will be what you will be able to spend. Next to take care of the costs, break your allowance. That is the money you bring into your emergency fund as you get down to the last $20. There will be no more until next week if the money is gone.

Allocate a percentage to go into a secret fund used exclusively for emergencies per payday. When it's time for the crunch, you'll know it's there.

Only to throw single dollar notes, set up one dresser drawer. This way, you'll have the singles handy when the pizza guy comes, and you won't need to split the bigger dollar numbers. This practice forces the mind to consider greater quantities and to conserve larger quantities. You're falling into the trap of just investing singles. It's working!

Bring just one card and pay it off per month in order to manage your credit card debt. The credit card moves into the safe where you only stash your emergency fund if you are tempted to overspend. You have a credit card you can use that will already be in good standing as crunch day arrives.

Jot down costs in a diary and count them and see whether you are above or under the spending figures at the end of each week. Put in more than you need, so that in case of a cash emergency, you still have a buffer.

It takes some time to watch your spending, but if you take good notes, you will still be able to see one or two places in which you are leaking cash. You will then come up with an additional $20 or more in savings each week. That's $1,000 a year for an emergency fund in real dollars.

More tricks to add to your own routine of savings:

Get your paycheck paid directly into savings rather than into your bank account immediately. You're going to pass funds to cover the bills, but you're going to worry twice about excess cash being withheld.

Allow one ATM withdrawal a week ONLY.

Immediately deduct the credit card transactions from your bank account, so that if the bill comes, you are not shocked.

Apply the number to the contributions you're currently paying to the next lender on your list as you pay off a debt. In case of a financial emergency, you should still transfer the money to a saving or savings account for a home, a holiday, or a new vehicle and this money will be made available.

Pay your Bills Online and Save

Nearly one-third of U.S. customers pay their bills electronically, says the leading supplier of electronic billing and payment systems, Judy Wicks of CheckFree.

Using a free, encrypted service provided by banks, credit unions, lenders, and companies such as AOL, MSN, Quicken, or Yahoo! is definitely the fastest way to pay your bills electronically. Arrange for an e-mail alert that a bill is due.

The service can manage payments completely online or if necessary, it can produce a paper check to pay the man who mows your lawn, for instance. If a payment is late, up to a certain amount (sometimes as much as $50), many bill-paying agencies will refund you with late payments as long as you have arranged the payment under their rules.

To shed still more documents, prepare online to collect bills and accounts. On multiple services or at MyCheckFree.com, sign up for e-billers.

The payment of online bills also lets you keep your money coordinated. Right there you have your documents, what you owe, past payments, and all on one platform.

Wells Fargo goes a little further: My Spending Analysis is open to its online banking clients, which they can use as a de facto budget. Online bill transfers and Wells Fargo debit and credit card charges are monitored by My Expense Report and plugged into one of 20 categories so you can see how much you have spent on, say, movies and restaurant meals.

Furthermore, of course, using Microsoft Money or Quicken, you can track your spending. With Quicken 2006, there's no need to print and file it until you pay a charge. Instead, you should connect the bill to the account from which you made the purchase online, so it is all at your fingertips.

Reward Yourself

Are you trying to find out which credit card is giving the best discount? The simple solution: take the money and run.

It should not have been better than this. You get either a check in the mail or a credit on your account for a cash refund, meaning you don't have to compare the competitive advantages of airline miles versus a new baggage collection. We streamlined the formula by estimating that you spend $33 per week on petrol, $100 a week on food, and $1,000 a month on other transactions to find the best prices.

The Citi Premium Platinum Select card (at. It costs 11.74 percent and provides 5 percent discounts on sales at supermarkets, drugstores, and gas stations and 1 percent for everything else. But in our example, Citi restricts its annual discount to $ 300, which you can hit in around eight months (you might move to another card at that point). Goods obtained through Citi's Dividend Merchant Network which includes more than 200 stores, catalogs, and blogs, are excluded from the limit. These sales offer discounts of between 5% and 7%.

Next up is the National City Daily Incentives Elite Visa card (at which our year-long shopping binge will receive a $270 refund. National City is unusual in bundling restaurants and food stores in a common category, with 2 percent rebates. The card discounts 4 percent on petrol, 3 percent on movies, and up to 1 percent on everything else with an interest rate of 10.49 percent, with an interest rate of 10.49 percent.

There is an interest rate of 11.24% on the American Express Blue Cash card (*www.americanexpress.com). It allows you up to 5% on grocery, petrol, and drugstore sales, and up to 1.5% on the remainder of your fees, up to $50,000 in gross spending. Complete rebate: $266 in our case.

With no dollar limit and a comparatively low 9.9 percent interest rate, the Capital One No Trouble Cash Card (at *www.capitalone.com) gives a discount of up to 3 percent on petrol and food and 1 percent on everything else you purchase. In our case, you'd receive an annual incentive of $237.

The Chase Free Cash Incentives Platinum Visa Card (at an interest rate of 11.99 percent) offers you one point (with a $60,000 spending cap) for every dollar spent on transactions. Furthermore, it has an odd twist: for any dollar, you spend in interest, a one-point bonus. You earn a check for $25 any time you accrue 2,500 points. You'd be eligible for a refund of $189 without the interest bonus, but the card is more appealing for card users who frequently hold a balance.

Several ways to reap the benefits of a Year-end Bonus

If you have a good chunk of extra cash to look forward to next year, imagine the right ways to bring it to use for you now.

Perhaps you'll get lucky this year. You've applied for the fantastic, higher-paying bonus, and your monthly salary would rise by $500. You just don't need to make sure the cash goes into creating a sustainable world rather than getting squandered on things.

It's one of the few ways to make a major difference in your life without trying to make sacrifices, which is the beauty of enjoying a year-end increase or bonus. And without modifying your current lifestyle, you've been living without money before, so you can take whatever financial medication you need.

Triage Financial

Next, remember that all the excess cash should be used to solidify the foundation first.

Next, all credit-card interest is paid off.

This will impact the remainder of the investments in a giant ripple. You'll have enough resources to commit to any other priorities as soon as you avoid paying higher interest charges per month.

If you don't already have three to six months' worth of living expenses in a secure, liquid account, pad your emergency fund. That way, when the biggest crises hit, you won't have to go into debt or steal long-term investments for unforeseen bills.

If you haven't reached the cap, add transfers to your 401(k). You will stop paying more taxes on the extra cash, and if you have an employer match, you can receive free cash. If you have not invested $3,000 in 2004 ($3,500 if you're 50 or older), you can still spend half of your bonus in your IRA. Using the incentive to make your 2005 IRA donation in January (the cap increases to $4,000 next year, $4,500 if you're 50 or older) or earmark a greater chunk of your gain per month if you've already hit the limit.

Taking a peek at the long-term debt that is

You have more options now that you've boosted your financial base. Watson is now in decent condition, but she also has over $17,000 in student loans dangling above her head, maxing out her 401(k) and Roth IRA savings. The loans have a low cost of 3.5 percent, so she's having to pick between adding $500 a month to her debt payments or saving the extra cash.

With interest rates so good, it doesn't need to be a priority to pay off the debt. Brian Jones, a certified financial planner in Fairfax, Va., says, "If you can earn at least 3.5% in the marketplace, and I think you can then investing is the better way to go." If you need to save for a short-term target, such as buying a home, saving becomes even more important.

It's all right, though, if you'd like to pay down a student loan to get it out of the way. "Psychologically, before you start moving forward, it's important to get these debts behind you," says Mari Adam, a professional financial planner in Boca Raton, Fla. "I know people who still have big loans in their 30s, and that debt becomes like a ball and chain around their legs."

If you're thinking of devoting part of your rise to making additional mortgage payments, the same is true. This year, Chris Crocket, a doctor in Tupelo, Miss., is receiving a big payout that might be able to pay off his debt with 4.75 percent left for 10 years. As long as his other foundations are secured, paying off the debt will give him the equivalent of a fixed return of 4.75 percent.

If you are going to retire prematurely or fear that you will lose your job, removing your mortgage payment will also help, says Evelyn D'Amico, a financial planner in Paoli, Pa. You don't want to tie up so much cash in a single investment, though. You may devote part of your increase or bonus to your mortgage for greater diversification and then spend the remainder.

Don't hesitate to make yourself a treat,

It's time for some fun to be had and you deserve it! You've been working hard to earn your bonus or boost, now go out and have some fun.

You should set up a fund for a holiday.

To pay for the vacation you have always needed, use part of your extra cash today. In a savings account paying 2 percent, you just need to put aside $310 per month to end up with $5,000 for springtime in Italy in 2006. Dream of enjoying spring in Italy! It will be a sort of holiday now.

Spend some of your home's income.

Most home renovations will save you a lot of cash over the long term. Think of the importance of storm-resistant windows and shutters, for instance. Spending an additional few thousand dollars today not only helps protect your house, but it will also increase its worth and decrease your homeowner's insurance premiums. This is intelligent preparation!

Starting up a charity fund is one final thought. You may set up a donor-advised fund of $10,000 at several mutual fund companies and investment firms. You will then automatically subtract the donations from the tax return and determine later which charities you would prefer to support.

A couple of Useful Savings Strategies

- For something that you can make or repair for yourself, don't spend a penny.
- Prolong the life of everything you own.
- Less use of what you like.
- Creatively thought. "Buy a new one" does not have to be the solution.
- If it can be reused or otherwise recycled, don't toss it.

These tried-and-true, pioneering principles, you should do now.

You can't just look for opportunities to invest now if you just want to save money. Today, you have to look at your life.

Basic Ways to Bring both Calm AND Savings to your Life

To save is much more than simply an action - it's a method of living, day-by-day.

Start to calm down by calming down first. Whatever it is you are now working on, abandon it. Spend a day in quiet and solitude for the next 30 minutes. In order to shift from the work-and-spend treadmill and then reflect on what is most important to you, you need to train your mind how to relax.

A heart that is peaceful is a tidy heart. It's time to get the act washed up. Start today by going through a wardrobe, a shelf, a drawer, and getting rid of something you don't need or cherish for 15 minutes every day. Weeding that out as you start on these surface areas, the knowledge and mentality transfer over to more nuanced areas such as the career, finances, and relationships.

Now it is time to learn what is appropriate. Being relaxed and safe is just about intentionally and purposefully changing your life. It decides what is sufficient in your life so that you can achieve much more in less.

Finally, if you're looking to save money or ease your life, seek some positive help.

Don't ever go alone. You are definitely not alone in your desire to save money, with Americans $2 trillion deep in debt. Find a mate who will help you get started and get busy afterward. You'll be happy you've done it.

In 6 simple moves, cut your electric bill

It makes very little sense to pay lots to save pennies, so if you're still on the lookout for a new appliance, count the Site as the first energy savings line of protection.

You could not have been so eco-conscious before the blinding bill of energy arrived in your mailbox. It's time to get the green in your pockets in mind and conserve resources at the same time.

Start by simply unplugging unused appliances, lowering the temperature to 120 degrees F on your electric water heater, and only washing maximum loads of dishes and drying them with air.

At the same time, take a peek at the free online calculators at Home Energy Saver, a U.S. funded website, to get personalized tips for enhancing the energy quality of your home. The Agency for Environmental Conservation (EPA) and the Energy Department (DOE).

It typically doesn't make sense to pay hundreds to save pennies, but if you're still on the market for a new appliance or even light bulbs, consider the Internet the first option for energy savings.

Contemplate climate management

According to the DOE's Energy Conservation and Clean Energy Network (EREN), an average household uses the majority of its energy for heating and cooling, up to 44 percent of the utility bill.

Mount a thermostat that is programmable. When no one is home or everybody is sleeping, this will minimize electricity lost when heating or cooling a house.

Energy Star programmable thermostats will save as much as 20 percent to 30 percent on your heating or cooling costs by allowing for several daily settings and automatically changing when the outdoor temperature changes, according to the Home Energy Saver blog. Honeywell, Hunter Fan, and Smart Systems International are among the participating producers. Unfortunately, searching for programmable thermostats according to Energy Star status is not simple. Instead, keep an eye out for those with Energy Star thermostat features that are typical: temperature recovery devices, two applications, and four temperature levels.

Remember fans of Ceiling

You start to be cooler as the breeze moves. This causes higher thermostat settings for summertime. The effect, according to EREN, is equal to reducing the air temperature by approximately 4 °F (2 C) and hence utilizing less energy than air conditioners.

Dream of lighting, cooking, and other appliances.

For illumination, heating, and other equipment, the next-largest household energy usage after temperature control is. This makeup about 33 percent of an average energy bill, not counting the fridge.

Think Fluorescent Compact Lamps (CFL's)

According to Home Energy Saver, CFL's will use up to 75 percent less energy than standard incandescent bulbs and will last up to 10 times longer. This is really positive because to start with, they're still more costly.

For inspiration, search your nearest utility. Look for a free "Conservation Kit" that contains two CFL's, among other items. This, of course, is an amazing deal!

Dream of energy-effective appliances

Search for Maytag washing machines by using the Energy Star site as a starting point. At Best Maytag, search for the Atlantis MAV9600 high-efficiency model for $689.

The refrigerator is likely your biggest energy user among household appliances, particularly if it's more than 15 years old. Up to 9% of the electricity expenditures alone can be paid for. Again if you're trying to substitute yours, check at the Energy Star site for a list of energy-efficient ones.

The Heating of Hot Water

Heating water is the third-largest expense of home electricity and usually accounts for 14%-20% of the average energy bill.

Think Hot Jackets for Water

Usually, hot water jackets retail for $10 to $20, and delivery costs will easily raise their cost by 50 percent or more when purchasing them online. To find offline deals in this situation, use the Internet.

Consider Aerating, Low-flow, and Showerheads Faucets

On a number of sustainability pages, including EnergyGuide, both Niagara and AM Conservation versions popped up, which still had the highest price at $6.75 for the four-way customizable Niagara showerhead. The good thing about buying from EnergyGuide is that depending on the ZIP code you enter, it instantly scans for any rebates.

You should prepare for energy conservation from the ground up for an energy-efficient homebuilding scheme while you're considering purchasing a new home. To locate projects close to you, search the DOE's Building America and the EPA pages.

Great WAYS TO FIND FREE MONEY

If you are tired of making improvements to your lifestyle to fit your savings goals, then read on. These reflections take you to prime locations to look for money that's rightfully yours already.

Any individuals find no sense in modifying their ways of saving a swift $5 or $10. It is daunting for these same persons to think that such small sums will potentially make a huge difference to their bottom line. They'd rather indulge in a little day-to-day luxury, like having an espresso cup every day than tighten their belts for what they see as measly savings.

Here are few realistic ways to save on items you are now paying for, for all the spendthrifts at heart. No reason to change your lifestyle, or at least your routines. Think of that as the money you are overpaying to someone now.

Move up and demand your free money on the tray!

Talk on a cell-phone

You figured it would take you 2,000 minutes a month, only to discover that 300 or even 200 would do just as well.

Ask to get the offer changed as soon as possible if you are coming to the end of your contract, or if the service provider can cancel the early-termination charge.

Think about this the 3,200-minute package for Verizon's America's Choice costs about $200 a month; you'll pay only $40 on the 400-minute plan for

America's Choice. This is provided that you don't begin to go over your minutes and pay costly overage costs, which is $160 a month in savings, or $1,920 a year. It will also cut your phone bill in half with an added $480 in your wallet, even shifting from America's Choice 1,100-minute package at $80.

Local and long-distance calling: If you don't spend all your cell-phone minutes on a package every month that doesn't encourage you to just roll them over with those otherwise-wasted minutes, you can at least cover your landline expenses. Are you doing that already? If you are consistently paying more than $50 a month, consider bundling your local and long-distance plans. Before taxes and fees, many packaged policies start at just $50 and encourage you to chat for as long as you want without the big bills.

However, measure all the above carefully. You would pay the same amount per month if your use is not constant, ensuring no exceptions for holidays when your use usually declines.

Your checking account: When was the last time you looked at your checking account's monthly fees calculated by your bank? You can spend much less money to escape higher rates by converting to a non-interest-bearing account.

Bankrate.com's annual checking account report finds that on interest-bearing deposits, average monthly fees are up to $10.86, vs. $3.72 for daily checking accounts. In order to avoid penalties versus the $245 minimum for the non-interest account, you would have to hold $2,258 socked out in the interest-bearing account. So what do you give up?

In the fall of 2003, at the time of the Bankrate survey, average yields sat at a paltry 0.27 percent. In the meanwhile, if you can, consider arranging withdrawals from your ATM. The total price you'll pay to use the ATM system of another bank is $2.69--$1.40 for the ATM bank and $1.29 for your own. It will save you a nice $140 per year by removing just one of these withdrawals per week.

Your policy: In a number of ways, you can save on your insurance premiums. Contact the insurance agent specifically for discounts: In addition to the regular decent college and auto policy protection incentives, if you insure more than one car, ask for a multi-product discount. When your car is worth less than $1,000, increase your deductibles on older vehicles or remove crash coverage entirely. According to Insure.com, raising your deductible from $200 to $500 will decrease your premium by as much as 30 percent.

NEVER overpay on your credit cards to borrow. If you think 2% or 3% isn't worth battling for on the APR of your credit card? Remember this: If you're an ordinary American, according to CardWeb.com's CardData Service, you owe $8,940 in household credit card debt. You can only spend $1,470 a year in interest alone at an estimated Avg of 16.44 percent.

You will save $89 for every 1 percent drop in APR. However, for the whole life of your mortgage, the difference is much more drastic. You spend $3,334 in net interest at the cheaper rate, figuring that you will make monthly installments of 5 percent of your loan each month. Nevertheless, you'll have billed $2,551 at an APR of 13.44 percent, which is 23 percent less.

Many cards even come with extra perks, such as airline miles or, best still even cashback. The Blue Cash Card of American Express credits you with up to 5 percent cashback; the GM card rewards 5 percent back for the purchasing or lease of a GM new vehicle. Which averages out to $447 on an average credit card balance of $8,940. To discover other low-rate and cash-back cards, use MSN Money's Credit Card Analyzer. In addition, for a rundown of the monthly benefits that credit cards provide, you can search CardWeb.

Your mortgage. The biggest financial option here is getting rid of PMI or private mortgage insurance. PMI protects the creditor should you default on your loan. You are obligated to pay this as long as the equity is under 20 percent, but once you hit the golden threshold, you will ask the lender to lower the charge.

The law specifically states that the lender must lower the fee if your equity exceeds 22 percent, provided that you have a conventional loan secured or refinanced after July 29, 1999, and you have a consistent payment history. However, if you have an older mortgage, without knowing it you might unnecessarily pay for this.

Depending on the size of your mortgage, this could add hundreds of dollars to the cost of your mortgage per month. Look at this now, now.

Get the best out of the available capital

Start by making use of what you have. Already paid for Internet access? An E-mail will be a perfect way to cut the telecommunications bills for long distances. It might not be a replacement for Dad's frequent heart-to-heart, but it should certainly be a substitute for When can we get together again?" "And calls. Why waste important cash on leaving voice mail?

Take the time to rid yourself of what you're not buying. If you're not using it when it's gone, you won't regret it. For a tax refund, recycle any unused products, hold a yard sale or sell them on eBay. It's time to remove the debt if you have to come up with the money for a storage unit with all that material.

Pay heed to future earnings

You may have had a hobby for years, but never thought about it as a money earner. Now take a close look at it. Try adding an ad in the document to show you how to do the same if you love to scrapbook. Develop a Web page at the same time where people will sign up to practice the craft online.

Could you just have old cash waiting to be claimed? You may have made a move and forgotten about an old bank account. There are plenty of free websites that list individuals that insurance agencies, banks, and services owe money to. Try CashUnclaimed and MissingMoney.

Ask for a discount

When you need to go out and buy a big-ticket piece, it is that time again. You may know how to shop around for the right discount, so you're about to ask for an offer. You've got your heart fixed on the ruby ring next time and you're ready to drop 3K to make the buy, pause, and think a bit about haggling the amount.

Making use of Good Commonsense and Planning - You Can Survive!!

Equipped with the funds which you have to endure, look to the below prospect lists and arm yourself, today, with all the supplies that you are going to need in a dreadful emergency:

Miscellaneous supplies to hold up

- twenty-five pounds' laundry soap · twelve twenty-eight oz. bottles of dish soap
- seventy-three rolls of toilet paper
- sanitary napkins in the adequate quantity
- eight gallons' bleach (used for sanitation and also laundry)
- twelve bars hand detergent · six twenty-four oz. bottles shampoo
- private items, like toothpaste, deodorant
- other things and chainsaw oil to keep things running
- pet foods
- livestock feed
- fifty-five gallons' kerosene for lighting
- twenty-five gallons Coleman gas or any other lantern gas

Suggested contents of a very good healthcare kit

- An excellent very first tool book
- Thermometer
- Everyday prescription meds for all family
- Antibiotics
- Ointments for the eye, cuts, and fungus
- Antidiarrheal medication
- Anti-Inflammatory medication as well as pain
- such as aspirin
- Burn therapy, like Burn Free
- Iodine/Betadine

- Alcohol
- Dental electrolytes (for dehydration from
- fever, diarrhea, stress)
- Frigid remedies
- Cough medicines
- Cough drops/throat discs
- Bandages
- Gauze
- Cotton
- Medical tape
- Scissors
- Hemostats
- Tweezers
- Needles to get rid of slivers
- A dental package to patch dentures, replace fillings, etc.)

<u>Checklist for stay-at-home emergencies</u>

- Food as well as water for the family, livestock, and pets for a minimum of fourteen days; fifty-five gallons of water that is new can last a family of 4 for more than 7 days.
- Daily medicines for the family for fourteen days
- Alternative heat supply & fuel
- Alternative making supply & fuel
- Alternative lighting supply & fuel
- Flashlights & batteries
- Transistor, crank, or perhaps sun radio
- Medical kit
- Matches
- Butane lighters
- Magnesium, flint & metal fire starter

Checklist for automobile crisis preparedness

- Jack & lug wrench
- Spare tire
- Shovel
- Electric battery jumper cables
- Fundamental application kit
- Fix-A-Flat
- Oil
- Lighter air pump
- A gallon of drinking water
- Blankets
- Basic very first aid kit
- Flashlight
- Emergency food
- Candles with matches
- Map
- C.B. or perhaps cell phone can be a lifesaver

Evacuation Needs

Storage food in big less hot #1

- Immediate potatoes
- Dried up milk
- Canned tuna
- Dehydrated eggs
- Dried up noodles
- Flour
- Shortening
- TVPs
- Dried up soup mixes
- MREs (military immediate Rice

- dishes; meals prepared to eat)
- Dried up beans
- Margarine powder
- Dehydrated fruit
- Dehydrated vegetables
- Tomato powder
- Baking powder
- Salt
- Spices & condiments
- Pudding mixes
- Cornmeal
- Instant coffee, tea, beverage mixes
- Sugar

Huge cooler #2

- Frying pan
- Huge pot
- Smaller pot
- Mixing bowl, steel (can be used as making utensil)
- Lighters and matches
- Bathroom paper
- Newspaper towels
- Dishtowel
- Dish soap
- Candles
- Dish scrubber pad
- Bowls for family
- Silverware for family
- Metallic spatula
- Roll of duct tape
- Small roll of wire
- Metallic cups for family

- Little h2o filter
- Propane stove & tanks
- Flashlight & batteries
- Hatchet

- Sleeping Gear (in a big clear plastic box) Sleeping bags
- Candles & lighters
- Coleman lantern
- An unopened gallon of lantern fuel
- Bow saw
- Bright socks & jackets
- 10' x 12' clear plastic tarp
- light tent
- Radio
- ammunition and Rifle/shotgun (food procurement, signaling, and family protection)
- Private backpacks
- Bright clothes
- Emergency food
- Socks
- Stocking hat
- Fundamental sport fishing gear with no rod
- Little very first aid kit
- Space blanket
- Flashlight
- Roll of rope and wire
- Pocket knife
- Canteen with cup
- Lighter
- A number of bucks in bills and quarters

BE PREPARED

www.ingramcontent.com/pod-product-compliance
Lightning Source LLC
Chambersburg PA
CBHW072032230526
45466CB00020B/1880